Quiet Love: .... eyes to see and words to tell the truths that are most true.

The Poems

Patricia A. Bow

Copyright © 2017 by Patricia Bow

All rights reserved

ISBN 978-0-9937857-8-8

Published by Patricia Bow

www.execulink.com/~thebows/patricia.htm

Distributed by Lulu Press

www.lulu.com

Contents:

Poems 1962-63	5
Untitled (Where do the birds go) January 1964	6
Rondeau Dec 1964	7
Winter 1967/68 1968	8
Like Haiku ....October 1968	8
By the Lakeshore ....January 1968	9
Untitled (Name) ....February 1969	10
Untitled poem (Nothing greener 1970	10
Untitled (Pregnancy) .... June 1971	11
Untitled (on Materialism) ....July 1971	12
Untitled (on November) ....Nov. 1971	13
Mark 10:17 - 25 ....January 21, 1972	14
Untitled (My love).... Valentine's Day 1972	15
Untitled (This is) .... February 1972	15
Mermaids ....Summer 1972	15
Untitled poem (My Child)....October 1972	16
Untitled poem (They used to say)....October 197	17
Father	18
The world is Round .... March 1974	19
Beatitudes ....August 1974	19
Basic ....Easter 1975	20
Untitled (End of Story) ....October 1975	21
Untitled Poem (In my garden) Jan. 1976	22
To R.V. ....February 1976	23
Untitled (Blue Hills) ....Feb. 1979	24
Nursery Rhymes 1980 -1981	25
12th Anniversary Poem (fragments) 1981	29
Fragments: Despair ....Nov 1982	30

Jamie at Ten and a Half ....Dec 1982	31
November .... 28 Nov. 1984	32
January Twilight .... January 1985	33
December Twilight ....Dec 1985	34

Poems 1962-63

---- I ----

Tonight the sky is less than pure,
And winds that fly across the towers
Stumble on stone, hard-shod, unsure.
The darkness drowns the quiet flowers

That glow less scarlet than before
I gave my heart and mind free rein
To gallop over valley and shore
And call up shadows of lasting pain.

Small spirits I cannot rebind
Rose up to haunt me, and I find
The devils that prompt me unawares
Are those I wakened with my prayers

---- II ----

Smooth blue canals and seas:
Bounding banks feathered
Dark-hearted clouds in fleets
Ragged and weathered

Last dregs of solid mist,
Edged round with lightning,
Sail on like pirate ships,
Straight to the brightening.

The round sun's radiant face:
Quick silver burning
White dazzle of his run,
Segmented, ferning,

Curling-up wisps of light
From the sun centre
Stiff-curve, from summer time
Drops to his winter.

Untitled (Where do the birds go) January 1964

Where do the birds go when the crush of winter
Plucks them from their foot holds on the rocks;
When winds in November call them off the cliffs,
Sweep them in fleets out from the coast at sunset?

Remember how compact they shone, last summer
Bright brown living birds, restless and content,
Now, drawn from the warm hollows by the sea's groaning,
The sky's leaning, and the deeply grasping cold.

How do they know where to go, when night has come down
When the waves burrow under the gale
Where do the birds go, when they mourn off this dim coastline.
And night gathers them, and all lights blow out?

Rondeau   Dec 1964

Do you wish to dam tight
This fast running river
And cage up forever
Blue herons in flight?

A fool with a fool's sight
Would linger forever
Would you cage herons white
and hold back the swift river?

Time has its own might;
Its fatal gifts never
Return to their giver
Would you cage herons tight?
Have you seen them in flight?

Am I   July 1965

Hair billows, whispers, shines
Edges glow with an unknown colour,
Growing like moonflowers out of a plain portrait.

I wish I were free like the swinging crystal,
School, shallow, shadows of the deep sea.

Winter 1967/68   1968

If I could achieve freedom
Like stiff seas bursting out of ice
I would do it.

If I could shatter the distance
Like glass,
Press months into a minute,
I would do it.

But the sea, even unfrozen,
Is contained by shores,
And I have not the strength to break them,
Nor the courage.

Like Haiku ....October 1968

Broken pewter sky
  gleams to greet me at dawn
    through red curtains.

The grey autumn beauty of towers
  watches the green dawn
    through grass blades.

By the Lakeshore ....January 1968

Among the ice
Brave bright ducks
Unsinkably bobbed_
This side of the break water,
A seeming submarine
Craggy with Atlantic ice.

Ice on the concrete shore,
Then grey crinkled blueness
Moving to the false horizon.

Like numbed yellow wine
The sun spread a stain to where
The unreal smoky silhouettes
Of faraway towns were
Featured, just above the horizon.

The boorish wind off the water,
The wind off the ice,
Was too cold, enveloping us
So small,
Two little castles
Hand holding and smoking cigarettes
And ambling.

We should have been crusted with frost,
As windows are on winter houses,
Small bubbles of happy heat
In a cold universe.

Untitled (Name) ....February 1969

What's in a name
      Baby frogs
        and polliwogs
   are the same.

Untitled poem (Nothing greener 1970

Nothing greener
Than my house in air
Squirrels and birds
None visit there.

Nothing greener
Than my mind in air
New born thoughts
Alone visit there.

Nothing greener
Than my eyes in air
Tree top visions
Alone come there.

Untitled (Pregnancy) .... June 1971

One month, you will be growing
Inside my body's night
In eight, I will be heavy
In nine, I will be light.

You now growing in my womb
Like a cloth upon the loom,
Secret, unborn mystery,
Soon shall lie for all to see
Perfect in your purity.

Stranger, son or daughter,
Are you dark or fair?
Well your head be darkly crowned
Or bright with angel hair?

Untitled (on Materialism) ....July 1971

I have dreamed of loneliness
In silence I have wished to be,
Striped of house, possessions,
Tied to holding, no-one, free.

Things to be kept and guarded,
Carpets, pictures on the wall,
All these things were meant to serve,
And now I serve them all.

To own too much can be a prison,
And I have dreamed of breaking free,
Hair, skin, eyes, alone and naked,
Riding the wind above a racing sea.

Untitled (on November) ....Nov. 1971

Ten o'clock in the morning,
 and all the streetlights on.
The windows round are full of lights.
This is the killing season,
better to be inside.

So short a time ago,
the sun crashed golden through the trees.
Now they are empty,
their fingers cold,
their glory trash.

Six months must pass
before we are warm again.

We muffle our faces
against the old enemy
who whispers, every killing season,
"One day, I will take the land back."

Untitled poem (on God?)
by Patricia A. Bow December 1971

Almighty God
dwelling in light
unapproachable,
how came you here
in the heart of this flower?

    Mark 10:17 - 25 ....January 21, 1972
I live in the soft prison of my desires,
home of all my comforts.
There is no other tenant,
and nothing breaks the silence.

Outside, in clarity of sun and wind,
God's voice reaches men
as well as angels,
hands touch,
and eyes look out for love.

I am a prisoner,
reaching no hands outward,
having withdrawn self to self.
Accustomed to my prison now,
I love it, fear to leave it.
     On being a librarian ....Feb 2, 1972

What of the green leaves seen
through the arched window?
Or the smell of green wet grass?

In my job I have to say no a lot.
I need a roof over my head,
this alone stifles rebellion.

A thousand pigeon holes and pettinesses
crowd in like black flies.
Is this my preparation for eternity?
If so, I'm hell ward bound.

　　　　　Untitled (My love).... Valentine's Day 1972
My love gave me five blossoms:
One
　　　kiss
　　　　　on
　　　　　　　each
　　　　　　　　　fingertip.

　　　　　　　　Untitled (This is) .... February 1972
This is the beauty of winter: at the end
when the crocuses come.

　　　　　　　Mermaids ....Summer 1972

Men go fishing constantly
and they fish mermaids from the sea.

Some men like the curving tail:
shining, fleshy, silver mail.

Some prefer the upper parts:
 maiden eyes, Madonna hearts.

So they cut the maids in twain,
Adding, "Fishes don't feel pain,"

and throw the rest - as the case might be-
flapping or screaming, back to the sea.

Men would be kinder to mer-females
If they could see their own tails.

Untitled poem (My Child)....October 1972

My Child, umbrelephant trees
grow wild in the antipodes,
so far from everywhere
my star can't journey there,
can't tell me how those trees
let swell and burst their seeds,
nor how their giant grace
shadows your distant face.

In Prison with you
by Patricia A. Bow October 1972

I tried to pick
the lock with my pen
but the pen
broke in my hand
and all its
blue blood dripped out.

So I used my head
instead
and I hypnotized
the guards

I am still here
but now I can
get out
 any time I like.

What stops me is
the fact
That you won't come.
And I know
you would be lonely.

Untitled poem (They used to say)....October 1973

They used to say,
        confine
your animal nature,
        refine
your baser instincts.

Now they say,
        define
your self-awareness,
        and mine
those deep unconscious riches

Still others say
        resign
yourself to nature,
become a little pattern in
        the Grand Design.

I say,
don't meddle with my id or ego,
        they're mine.
Don't offer me
a partnership with death,
I won't
        co-sign.

Father
(August 25, 1908 - April 19, 1973)

You never left us so before:
suddenly,
with no goodbye,
without a word of your return.

The master of ceremonies
tried to persuade us
you were the one lying silent
in a room heavy with flowers,
The only actor without a speaking part.

I knew you were not there.

Others, with faces solemnly arranged
(so unlike your own)
told us you were gone
to realms
golden with angels, eternally serene.

That may be so; I don't know.
Such distant joys seem less real
than what I see in your brothers' faces,
hear in your children's voices:
Shared looks, laughter inherited.

The world is Round .... March 1974

If the world were flat,
no matter where you start
you'd surely find an ending,
a place to part.

But the world is round
and we two are one:
Our story will be endless,
like the journey of the sun.

Beatitudes ....August 1974

Blessed are the white: for they shall lay waste the earth.
Blessed are the black; for they shall suffer greatly.
Blessed are the brown: for they shall man factories at
lower wages.
Blessed are the red: for they shall be despoiled, and then
neglected.
Blessed are the yellow: for they shall be ever resourceful,
and ever suspect.
They say the races are mingling.
In ten thousand years, what colour will the children be?
Blessed are the beige: for they shall inherit the earth.

Basic ....Easter 1975

I love you little more than I love air
for every time I draw a breath
a puff withstands the void of death:
I love you little more than I love air.

I love you little more than I love water.
It sends the new green springing high,
without it I would surely die;
I love you little more than I love water.

I love you little more than I love bread.
It binds the muscle to the bone,
it sends the heartbeat throbbing on;
I love you little more than I love bread.

Untitled (End of Story) ....October 1975

End of a story afternoon,
  bitten off and swallowed by November.
   The elms have an ancient, deaf and
       brittle look,
  windless, their tangles too braided
   to be stirred.

  Light gathers,
   bleeds colour upwards in the west.
  Dark gathers,
   thickens like smoke in the streets.
  Night pursues,
   and streetlights leap like moons
    out of the air.
   Across the street visitors ring,
    and the drowsy house
    opens a golden eye.

Untitled Poem (In my garden) Jan. 1976

In my garden I will grow
baby's breath and bergamot
fearless of all winds that blow,
so secure they'll shelter there.
Marigolds and maidenhair
in the borders I will sow:
roses and anemones,
and all gentle plants like these.

In my garden I can find
lilacs of the deathless kind,
hollyhocks and columbine.
Summer there will never end,
blackening frost will not descend,
where my garden's fences wind,
through the meadows of my mind.

Every morning you pass through,
 leaving footprints in the dew.

And at night, you and I,
arm in arm, walk quietly.

To R.V. ....February 1976

Yesterday, while walking
in the Rosedale Ravine,
I met a person of doubtful parentage:
part man, part horse.
He asked me if I had seen
any centauresses hereabouts.
I gave him your address.

This morning, while walking
beside the Humber River,
I met a man who was also
a fish.
He asked me if I had seen
any mermaids in these waters.
I referred him to you.

Let me know if either
of these characters
looks you up.
I thought you might be
pleased to meet them,
you being of similar bifold nature:
part girl, part woman,
convent eyes and carnival laugh,
walking with care
through the leafy shadows
and sunlight of your mind.

Untitled (Blue Hills) ....Feb. 1979

The blue hills across the river
are distant as death,
unattainable as clouds.
To reach them, you must
see winter burn
in the early morning air,
hear the shine of icicles. You have to drown yourself
in sunlight. And none of our citizens
has ever dared.

To James, on Graduating from Grade 3 ....June 1981
When you grow up to be a man,
you'll be a mathematician,
or else you'll be a physicist
and go out nuclear fission.

Maybe you'll be a poet:
a poet is someone who
has eyes to see and words to tell
the truths that are most true.

Or maybe you'll be a journalist
and brighten up the Star
or maybe you'll be on the T.T.C.
and drive the Queen Street car.

Perhaps you'll seek the Why
behind cosmology,
and put the answer in a box,
and bring it home to me

Nursery Rhymes 1980 -1981
I

Jamie had a nasty cough
When he was five years old.
I went to buy some medicine,
but all of it was sold.

So I told him a story
about a boy so bold,
Who folded all the darkness up
and turned the night to gold.

II

What if dandelions
really were
dandy lions?

Then pussy willows would meow,
tiger lilies would roar,
and dogtooth violets
would bite.

III

I see shells on the seashore.
I see ships and fishes.
I share my lunch with porpoises,
and then I do the dishes.

IV

Rain, rain, go to Spain.
Go to Gander or Spokane.
Go and rain on Washington
Jamie wants to see the sun.

V

Have you seen the man in the moon?
Yes I have seen him.
Sometimes he looks happy,
Sometimes he looks sad.
I like him best when he's glad.

Have you seen the woman in the sun?
No, I've never seen her.
Inside her house of fire
She hides herself all day
and when I look, she makes me look away.

Have you seen the people in the stars?
No, but I've heard them.
They sing in the dark
When I turn out the light,
and answer me when I say goodnight.

VI

Fire engine, fire engine in the night,
you sound so lonely far away.
You're not at all as you were today,
when the sun made all your brass shine bright
and the station flag was flying.

Now it's dark and I'm in my bed,
and it's hard to remember how brave and red
you looked when I met you today.
Your siren sounds like somebody crying;
you sound so lonely far away.

VII

See you later
alligator

    After while
    crocodile

Run the bath
tall giraffe

    Scrub your toes
    bells and bows

Toss the towel
snowy owl

    In the loo
    Kangaroo

Find pyjamas
wild bananas

    Brush your teeth
    Indian chief

Now to bed
Punkinhead

    kiss and hug
    cuddle bug

Snuggle down
silly clown

    Douse the light
    say goodnight!

VIII

In springtime, when your birthday comes,
and gardens change old clothes for new,
and young birds start to learn old tunes,
then I will be a friend to you.

In summer, when cicadas call,
and golden mornings set us free
and every night is magical,
then you will be a friend to me.

In fall, when ragged trees begin
to throw off leaves in windy weather,
and moon grows fat and sun grows thin,
then we will be good friends together.

In winter, when the year is old
and night grows long at either end,
and all the sidewalks crunch with cold,
we still will be each other's friend.

12th Anniversary Poem (fragments) 1981

I know the scent and shape of you:
I know you all, yet not at all.
I linger with a connoisseur's delight
over a contour of bone, a texture of skin,
gloating over treasures of silk and ivory
that are mine alone,
and yet no-one's but yours.

For you and I are so entwined
that we can read each other's mind
at times, a simple exercize.
Then comes the stumble of surprise
when, reaching out in haste, I find
the stranger self behind your eyes.

Far apart upon the lawn,
two tall trees confront each other
never to touch, ever alone:
yet beneath the grass and stone
intertwined their roots have grown,
so intimately webbed together,
neither one can tell his own.

So with us: which flatly proves
futility of arguments
On which is which, and whose is whose.

Fragments: Despair ....Nov 1982

The world turns, turns
into darkness.
All the bright cities
slide into shadow,
the sweet green fields
turn grey, leprous.

We perceive the light
only as it fades.
We listen for the children
after hearing of their murder.

Where are the ones who sleep their days
in silent, healing harmonies,
balm to our wounds?

Where are the ones who measure out
the poetry of secret prayer,
who link the shattered times
with perfect rhymes?

Where are the blessed?
All dead centuries ago?

Mother Theresa, have I gone blind,
or have the furies blown
your candle out?

Jamie at Ten and a Half ....Dec 1982

For you, the world is magical.
rainbows, golden windows,
shadows lurking in the corner,
all on the edge of sight.
All real.

The magic is in you, and in your eyes.

You look upon me, looking up
and see a woman
wise, strong and beautiful:
a queen.

Not long now till the day
when magic fades, outgrown;

And you, through eyes
suddenly alert and clear
will see

me.

November .... 28 Nov. 1984

October past, like vital middle age,
quicker than thought or expectation gone,
November storms upon us, lean and wan,
all silvered, like King Lear upon the stage.
It's growing old that sets him in a rage:
 the grief of losing life, of moving on
before his business properly is done.
They snatched the book before he'd filled his page.

November's tears, like stones against the glass,
bite bitterer than summer's velvet rain.
The green blood bleaches from the tattered hill,
the red from wrinkled cheeks; he thinks of pain,
of icy sleep. Then takes up hope again,
recalls the Resurrection, and is still.

January Twilight .... January 1985

Footprints in the snow: wild wolfish prints
that conjure images of savagery.
I tracked them as a child, have lost them since,
abandoned chase for domesticity.

Here on this waste- fences like forest walls -
white sheets are torn across by vicious claws,
the same that strike my face. The snow that falls begins to
blur the marks of giant paws.

Behind the fences, only half concealed,
the ogres crouch, their hungry eyes a gleam;
Beneath pale fur their glittering fangs revealed,
their hot breath blown in sideways gusts of steam

I see them, and am not seen: the loneliness
of he who watches, is alone, is free,
armours me with magic. In this dusk
only the great wolf is aware of me.

The track is clear - too clear: an ancient game.
the hunted has remembered how to chase.
The beast still lives, and knows my name.
He'll challenge when I meet him face to face.

December Twilight ....Dec 1985

The sky, a cry of crimson,
has faded to a glow,
and winter for his citizens
has lit the lamp of snow.

It shines like creature under sea,
or phosphorescent ghost,
or secret slow corruption,
or heaven's icy host:

Yet never sheds its light on me,
for I am Adam's child,
and we were never meant to see
a light so pure and wild.

Such a light, so cold, so rare -
sheen of sapphire, gleam of pearl-
surely wells from other worlds,
where griffins ride the lambent air

to prey on princely wanderers, who
pursue their quest in vain,
while snow-white unicorns lie unseen
upon the velvet plain.

www.ingramcontent.com/pod-product-compliance
Lightning Source LLC
Chambersburg PA
CBHW032114040426
42337CB00040B/704